Stratford upon Avon

A little souvenir

CHRIS ANDREWS PUBLICATIONS

Stratford
upon
Avon

Introduction to Stratford

Stratford ('street across the ford') was a river crossing in Roman times. Two Anglo-Saxon settlements later joined to become a market in 1196. It thrived as a busy market town, and at the time Shakespeare was a child his father the mayor welcomed groups of actors to entertain the townspeople. This may have started Shakespeare's interest in theatre, which led him to London to work, but he returned to Stratford near the end of his life. The town enlarged significantly during the sixteenth century when Edward VI granted its charter and agriculture grew, though the Shakespeare connection accounts for much of its current business.

William Shakespeare was born at the building now known as 'The Birthplace' in Henley Street in 1564, he died in 1616 on the same day - April 23rd, and was buried in Stratford's Holy Trinity Church. At eighteen he married Anne Hathaway from the small village of Shottery and some

Shakespeare's Birthplace and the Shakespeare Centre in Henley Street   5

6   Holy Trinity Church

five years later they moved to London. William worked at the Globe Theatre and probably appeared on stage in small parts. He began writing plays in the 1590's and produced some 38 in total, 18 of which were published in his lifetime, *Love's Labour's Lost* and *The Comedy of Errors* being amongst the earliest with *The Tempest* as his last complete play.

Shakespeare is acknowledged as England's greatest poet and playwright and, though he wrote nothing about his actual birth town, his life and work remains inextricably entwined with Stratford.

Anne Hathaway's Cottage

10 Palmer's Farm at Wilmcote

Sculptures in the Bancroft Gardens

12   William Shakespeare's Birthplace in Henley Street

The Birthplace garden in summer   13

14   The back of Shakespeare's Birthplace

Early morning view in Henley Street   15

16 The Gardens and Birthplace

Front and back doors of The Birthplace   17

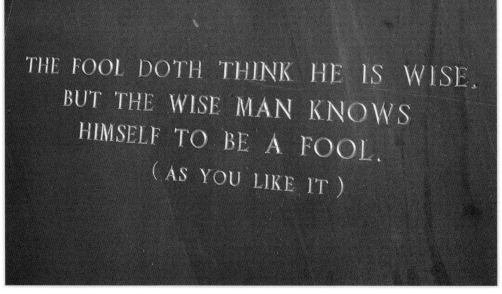

THE FOOL DOTH THINK HE IS WISE,
BUT THE WISE MAN KNOWS
HIMSELF TO BE A FOOL.
(AS YOU LIKE IT)

18   Inscriptions and sculptures recording Shakespeare's work are in many places in the Town

20   Holy Trinity Church, the River Avon and The Royal Shakespeare Theatre

The Church in spring and autumn

22 The bust of William Shakespeare and his grave in Holy Trinity Church

The High Alter
and stained glass
in The Church

The River Avon, Church and entrance to the Bancroft Garden moorings

26   Canal boats at the moorings

28 Mute swans are common on the river and nest in Bancroft Gardens

Clopton Bridge and hire boats at dawn 29

The River
Avon and
Stratford from
the east
30

Weir on the Avon below the Church   31

32 Morning mist

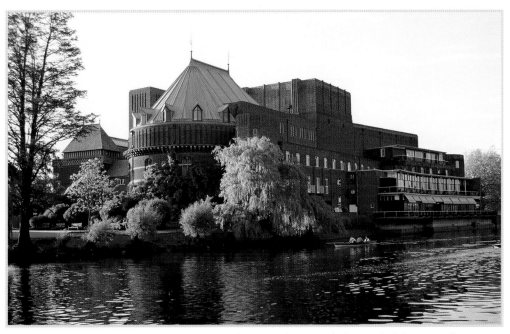

34   The Theatre at dusk

36   Exhibition at 'The Falstaffs Experience' museum

Water sculpture in the gardens at the theatre and the memorial donated by an American to Stratford   37

38   Some of Stratford's oldest houses

42   The Pub named after David Garrick, noted actor and founder of The Shakespeare festival in 1769

Stratford's busy streets have a good variety of shops and restaurants   43

44   The Grammar School where Shakespeare studied, still a school today

The Town with the Chapel, Nash's House and New Place and their gardens   45

46 Nash's House and New Place

The Chapel and the rear of Nash's House with the knott garden. 47

48   The Herb Garden and Hall's Croft

50   Shottery with Anne Hathaway's Cottage

Anne Hathaway's Cottage, the pre-marital home to Shakespeare's wife   51

52   The garden and Cottage in spring

The Cottage is a twelve roomed Elizabethan farmhouse 53

54 Autumn, the view from the orchard

56   Mary Arden's House and Palmer's Farm at Wilmcote

The Mary Arden site comprises two sixteenth century farmhouses and a Countryside Museum   57

58 Mary Arden's house in early spring

Mary Arden was Shakespeare's mother and lived here before marriage 59

60 Falcons on a cadge at the Birthplace Trust's Shakespeare Countryside Museum

62 Palmer's Farm was a working farm all its life

The half timbered buildings are little altered over the centuries 63

First published 2005 by
Chris Andrews Publications 15 Curtis Yard North Hinksey Lane Oxford OX2 0NA

Telephone: +44(0)1865 723404 email: chris.andrews1@btclick.com.

Photos by Chris Andrews with additions from Phil Ruler

ISBN 1 905385 01 3

www.cap-ox.com

ACKNOWLEDGEMENT

Many thanks to the Shakespeare Birthplace Trust for their encouragement and kind permission to show their many aspects. The inclusion of a building or view in this work does not necessarily indicate a right of public access. Text and design by Chris Andrews, Origination by Butler and Tanner, Printed in Singapore.

Front Cover: Anne Hathaway's Cottage
Title: Sculpture in The Great Garden
Back cover: Palmer's Farm